Photographed by the author

REFLECTIONS
Rhyme and Reason

Omar H. Malik

authorHOUSE®

AuthorHouse™ UK
1663 Liberty Drive
Bloomington, IN 47403 USA
www.authorhouse.co.uk
Phone: 0800.197.4150

Published by AuthorHouse 04/27/2016

ISBN: 978-1-5246-3171-0 (sc)
ISBN: 978-1-5246-3170-3 (e)

Print information available on the last page.

I dedicate this book to my four grandchildren
Jessica, Annabelle, and twins Kailen and Malika.

CONTENTS

POETRY IN MOTION

An expression of emotion,
Of words in animation,
A philosophical message,
An allegorical passage,
An observation captured,
In lucid language pictured,
An enlightened literature,
A chronology of culture,
A reflection of life and time,
Expressed in rhythm and rhyme.

22.12.2013

REFLECTIONS

Earth's eternal journey through space
On a path not marked, leaving no trace,
Following a fixed imaginary orbit,
Orbit repeating an annual circuit,
A timeless, ceaseless celestial journey,
Solar secrets hiding a vital key.

Inhabiting this electro-magnetic sphere,
Curious, is any one in outer space there?
Matter, energy, fertility and mortality,
Beauty, love, knowledge and ambiguity,
Abstract energy and emotions,
Physical existence and erosions.

An audio-visual synchrony of consciousness,
Perceptions and conceptions five senses harness;
Darkness and light, night and day, clock creation,
Relativity, gravity, light, space, time and motion –
Images and imprints uniquely defined
In reflections in the mirror of mind.

21.05.2014

AWAITING IN ANTICIPATION

Poems are like flower buds
Dormant in the core of mind
Waiting for time measured
Sunshine and showers to whisper,
Then, slowly waking up in bloom.
I await in anticipation
That my mind one day
May bloom and blossom
In lucid language and expression
Revealing a clear reflection
In the mirror of my mind.

21.11.2015

A LEAF'S LEASE OF LIFE

In Spring, embellished in bloom seen,
In Summer, wore bright breezy green,
In Autumn, a divinely painted hue,
Final parting hour ruefully in view;
After howling wind's tease and torment
Trying hard to hang on to the last moment.
Following release, a last dance,
Singing the finale in a trance,
Rustling through the whirling wind,
Finally, buried in a heap of own kind.
In Winter, evergreens stay firm and defy
Frost, snow and chill wind's howling cry.

20.11.2014

A POTENT POWER

Money, money, money, a popular cry,
Then, spend, spend, spend and buy, buy, buy,
Money merrily chasing galloping greed
Blinkered, by-passing contentment's need.

Scholars proclaim knowledge is bliss try, try, try,
Time tearing through life, destined to die,
Catching time for the loved ones, priceless, can't buy!
Blessings of good health money's inadequate to quantify.

Mountains of money, an abstract, in dwarf measure,
Looking high up to love, life's gift and greatest pleasure,
Happiness bought is fraught with temptation wilderness,
Guise of charities squeezing the heart of kindness.

Watching a spoilt sport, money, robbing all sporting spirit,
Fine arts coy, core compromised by pop arts, consumer fit.
Life's best gifts can boast, they are beyond money's measure,
A purity of feeling, simple, yet, achieves heightened pleasure.

Life time, priceless and finite, phased out of money's eye,
Creative time, leisure time, idle time, till time waves good bye.
Money, though, materialised as a mere medium of exchange,
Proved potent, intoxicating power, no bounding range.

A power, volatile, equal affinity to good action and evil flirtation,
A power, a beacon of light, of goodness in sight for action,
A power, prone to perilous, mindless hollow consumption,
A power, constantly changing hands since it's origin and conception.

02.09.2014

ANGER

When devil's advocate wilfully plead
I try very hard not to heed,
Then, at a moment's slip
I am in his strongest grip.

Gripped into a veronal volition,
In an inane emptiness of reason,
Thrown into an unsobering rage,
Potentially powerless to disengage.

Some misguided view of anger
An impression of being the stronger;
How can I be stronger losing control,
Devil's advocate robbing harmony's soul?

I feel I am forced into changing my face,
Forced into devil's mask of disgrace,
Resorting to tarnished vocabulary,
I rather be in control and conciliatory.

Fiendish dark emotions riding high,
A fallible blinding vision reasons defy,
Families and friends fall out and falter,
Decisions in anger not allowed to alter.

A false pride or an ill conceived honour avenge,
A vendetta, a tit for tat retribution or a revenge,
Devastating consequences in rabid rendition,
Devil's delight in a beguiled apparition!

Larking to lure, pervious to pretend,
Not revealing true colours of a fiend,
Disguised, waiting to strike given chance,
This shadow of a swarthy countenance.

02.10.2014

ANIMAL INSTINCT

Big fish surviving eating the small,
Small plant is suffocated by the tall,
King of the jungle starved without his prey,
Natural process humans powerless to disobey.
Long left the brutal land of the jungle,
Life remains a process of survival and struggle,
Ceaseless slaughter of animals for consumption,
Human killing fields of unstoppable wars of destruction.

In the deep jungle of macro-economic affluence
Capitalism's credibility in greed fuelled nuance;
King of the jungle enjoying lion's share in opulent dens,
Jobless queues at food banks and soup kitchens,
Homeless seeking refuge in cold filthy street corners,
'Fat cats' cushioned and warm, they are high earners;
Establishment in collusion at best in economic illusion,
Political masters seeking power by rhetorical profusion.

Many parts of the world in war torn habitation,
Many born facing stark prospect of starvation,
Others in an orgy of over consumption and waste,
Enough to fulfil dream of a fair share still in quest.
Power of greed overwhelming the strongest,
Laws of the jungle heeding survival of the fittest,
Even with a rational mind and power to reason,
Succumbed to animal instinct, blinding a noble vision.

11.10.2014

ANSWER IS THERE IS NO ANSWER

Holding one way ticket to an earthly mission
Or, on a testing return journey in transition;
Prophets assured, enlightened by revelations,
Religions preaching their respective versions.

Believers comforted by a peaceful sanctity,
A way of life, social fabric and fraternity,
Inter religion animosity and intolerance
Violating sanctity and it's holy core essence.

Negotiating cross roads of good and evil,
Love and hate, shadows of the devil.
Radiance of beauty, charity and benevolence,
Overshadowed by ugliness of insolence.

Misty mazes of conflicting choices,
Many speeches, many assertive voices,
Answers hidden in riddles and darkness,
An earthly goal of survival, peace and happiness.

What purpose in this temporal passage on earth
In allocated spells of misery and mirth?
Paradoxes and riddles closely conferring,
Seeking answers humans repeatedly erring.

Decisions hardly ever made clear cut,
Hiding in a hollow haze of ifs and buts,
Nothing leading to a path certain,
Only, death's call for final curtain.

Truth twisted and tormented in acts of perjury,
Falsehood claiming credence in veiled illusory,
Right revolving in a dual core of perception,
Wrong's abject aberration seeking absolution.

Three life defining truths vowing,
That the sun will rise every morning
And will be setting every evening;
Time draws curtain for every living being.

Origin obscured, end points towards eternity,
Space and dimensions inferring infinity,
Philosophers and scientists at wits end,
In constant quest for knowledge to comprehend.

16.12.2014

AUTUMN

As the Summer sun bids goodbye
Woodland trees begin to sigh!
Mild sun kissed leaves gently fade
Into glorious Autumn shade.

Losing Summer's green lush,
Colours painted by a divine brush
In rustic red, bronze and golden yellow,
Shaken by chill wind's cruel blow.

Floating and falling in gentle breeze,
Descending slowly, dancing at ease,
Falling leaves leaving bare bough trees
Facing Winter's wrath, frost and freeze.

Wild life getting busy at nature's call,
Adapting to changes seasons install,
Migrating birds busy in preparation,
Others homing in on hibernation.

Autumn equinox negotiating the sun
For shorter appearance in daily burn,
Sun losing height, casting longer shadows,
No grazing cattle in misty meadows.

Seems not long when Spring was here,
Now howling wind ripping trees bare,
Few lonely leaves try longer to hang
From same boughs birds in Summer sang.

22.10.2014

BEAUTIFUL GIFT OF NATURE

As I wake up one Spring morning,
The sun at day break, as promised, rising,
Serenaded by sweet sound of dawn chorus,
Clouds give way and gently fly pass
And as the passing clouds keep flying by
In a wave unveiling a deep blue sky.

As the sun's gentle, whispering, awakening ray
Shines and shimmers on calm and tranquil bay,
Sparkling on fresh Spring leaves on trees anew,
Sparkling on delicate flower petals set in pearl due,
On clear water springs, rippling rills and rivers too,
A new day is born and begins to live through.

As the day ends and the sun is setting down to rest,
The moon rise to the occasion and smiles at her best,
Floating clouds, at times, stealing her moments and
defy
And as I gaze in amazement at the star studded sky,
In a transcending moment I reflect and revere
Creation's beautiful gift of nature.

30.05.2014

BEAUTY IN TIMEFORM

When I look at flowers I see
Flowers smiling at me
In beautiful blushing bloom
Transforming shadows of my gloom.

Behold a beautiful baby newborn
Like beautiful sunrise each morn,
Enjoy the simplicity and purity
Before contamination corrupts beauty.

When time robs little girl's innocent childhood
At time's threshold, stepping into womanhood
Like flower buds burst into blooms
Enchantment of youth as beauty blossoms.

When a caterpillar transforms
By metamorphosis of life forms
Into a beautiful colourful butterfly
Time transforming beauty's eye.

For ruffle- feathered grey cygnet
Time choosing a magic moment
Enrobing in a pure white apparel
Turning into a beautiful swan in a spell.

Fathom the dark hollowness of night
Followed by brightness of daylight,
Beauty of blue sky, warm air when sunny
Or, even when cloud covered and rainy.

Weather permitting, gaze into a star studded night,
Silvery moon's happy face or shy as it might
Or, dark clouds forming, tempest brewing,
Many faces of beauty nature renewing.

Looking into natures every loom
Beauty transforming temporal gloom,
Texture and tapestry of colour and light,
Interplay of time in beauty's sight.

11.11.2015

BIRDSONG

Migrating birds homeward bound,
Following hushed Winter nature's awakening sound,
Harbinger of Spring blowing trumpets fanfare on arrival,
Trees adorned in green, embellished in revival.

Incipient gleam of dawn to daybreak
Celebrating sunrise as the earth awake,
Polyphony of mirth and merriment in the air
Heralding sound- sweetened spring fair.

Plucking strings of Spring's lyre and lute,
Passerine's melodic harp and flute;
Voices of Spring in sweet serenade
In an ensemble of pure lyrical cascade.

Hymns to the sun by perched passerine
On arched branches of woodland, green,
In an oasis of calm and tranquillity,
In a wave of pure melodic spirituality.

Blackbirds, thrushes and nightingales
Singing merry melodies of seasonal tales,
Singing solo or in a chorus in total harmony,
Adding floral colours in a choral symphony.

I hear nature's orchestra play,
Nature's enchanting choral display,
Birds of feathered beauty copiously feature
In this seasonal musical offerings from nature.

14.04.2014

BLUEBELLS

In a hush woodland vale,
Bluebells under Springs spell,
Caressed by a gentle breeze
In lush blue hue, dancing at ease
Like the wave of a deep blue sea
Under a woodland canopy.
Windswept, whispering in a spree,
Rays of Spring sunshine in glee,
In light and shade bound,
In laughter without sound,
Playing hide and seek
In a silent language they speak.

21.05.2015

BULL FIGHT

Waiting for actions to commence,
Spectators in anticipation arrive,
Bullring full, humming, set alive,
Matadors and toreadors tense.

Attired in traditional apparel,
'dressed to kill'
Apparitions fitting the bill,
Crowd expecting heroes to excel.

Bull let loose, confused in fright,
Sees red, cautiously tread and charge,
Spectators dread, fearful, emotions surge,
Fight commence at crowd's delight.

Life's at stake, man against beast,
An echoing arena in the round,
A mixture of gasping and roaring sound,
A blunt and brutal sporting tryst.

Glory gathered in hands blood stained,
Crowd left ecstatic and entertained.

28.05.2014

BUS STOP

I am looking at a bus stop and as eyes behold
I see a live drama begins to unfold.
Curtains raised, in a creative motion,
Moving in a forward direction,
Man and machine in a joint traction,
Visions of varied agenda and action;
I am witnessing a short episode
Of their life's journey as yet untold.

Passing images of many faces in framed windows,
Men, women, boys and girls sitting in rows,
Some cell-phone in hand talking or texting,
Some engrossed in games perplexing,
Some sitting up some crouched,
Some interested in what's around,
Some absorbed in deep thought,
Some seem fearful and fraught.

Faces happy and cheerful,
Faces sad and tearful,
Faces of favourable outcome and expectation
Faces of fear of the unknown and apprehension.
Drama I watch one by one unfold,
Drama I watch, but, words not told,
Drama not portrayed by actors,
Drama of real life characters.

25.03.2014

COLOURS

A golden glow in the far east horizon each morning,
I open my eyes at sun rise to a colourful life unfolding,
Seven colours of spectrum compressed in sun's radiant rays
Feeding life into all earthly colours each proudly displays.

Imagine, at the origin, when the earth woke up in the
early hours,
It was granted a divine brush stroke of chosen colours;
Sky screening the heaven wished to be painted blue,
Lakes, rivers, seas and oceans desired to reflect parallel hue.

Plants in forests, woodlands, meadows and valleys all green,
Sun wore a golden crown, moon a silvery sheen,
Rainbow reflected seven colours that sun impregnated,
Cloud wore white, then, many shades of grey precipitated.

Mountains merrily chose scraggy grey or volcanic ash brown,
Some sheltering green vegetation others in snow capped
crown,
Birds, butterflies and tropical fishes allowed abundant dyes,
Some animals camouflaged, confusing predators' eyes.

King of the jungle, arrogantly, displaying golden brown
mane,
In animal world, white, grey, black, brown, striped or
spotty stain.
Flowers, finally ordained, queen of all shades of colours,
Adorned, robed and crowned in life long glittering hours.

A blonde or a brunette, eyes blue or brown, rosy lips and
cheeks,
Colours glow and shine when a woman in her height of
youth peaks.
With paints palettes, canvas and brushes of inspirations
Natural vivid colours captivate and capture artists'
imaginations.

Human lifestyle creating counterfeit colours dare
Ideas borrowed, as nature quietly stare
At painters' palettes and colouring brush stroke
And computer generated colours bespoke.

Colours in nature, colours in boudoirs and bowers,
Colours in gardens, colours in wild flowers,
Colours in attires, colours in manners,
Colours in cars, colours in banners.

Colours bright and beautiful, but, not fed and fade at night,
Starved and subdued without the life-line of luminous light,
With the lustre of light, colours beautiful and bright unfold
Into a colourful world, oh yes, 'tis a colourful world – behold!

01.10.2014

DAFFODIL

Daffodil, Daffodil
Sing, soundless, if you will
Daffodil, Daffodil
Dance, doubtless, you will.

Following Winter's repose
In early Spring you arose,
Windswept you dance
In a captivating trance.

As soft sunshine embrace
Your whispering grace,
Your golden yellow face
Glowing in seductive caress.

Haloed harbinger of Spring
What joy and delight you bring;
Spring fever on earth fuelling
In all living hearts dwelling.

Daffodil, Daffodil
My heart with joy you fill,
Daffodil, Daffodil
Stay a little longer if you will.

01.03.2016

DARK ALLEY

The fear of burning hellfire
Failing to dent or deter devil's dare
Yet, lured by the promise of heaven
Followers of faith are strongly bedriven.

But, the dead alley is dark, very dark!
No light, not even a single spark;
No traveller ever came back and revealed
The truth, unfathomed, remains eternally sealed.

18.08.2014

DARK CLOUD

Shrouding the sun, gathering dark cloud,
Thunder and lightning enjoying singing loud,
Dark rain cloud responding to earth's call for moisture,
Rain feeding springs, lakes, rivers, plants and pasture.
'Dark cloud' sun worshippers unloved adage
For heaven sent life saving messenger in camouflage.

Apparent dark side, occasional lack of skill,
Overenthusiastic and a tendency to overfill,
Just as the mighty sun may at times overkill
Like the deserts of Sahara, barren, standing still.
Dark cloud breathing life in drops of rain,
Dark cloud holding the rein travelling not in vain.

Answering farmers' prayers with timely rain drops,
Rain clouds feeding the world with seasonal food crops.
As every dark cloud comes with a silver lining,
In dictum silver lining is earth's survival defining,
On arrival met an earth scorched and ailing,
Leaving behind sun shining again and earth smiling.

26.11.2015

DAY BREAK

That moment when night and day meet,
When sun begins to rise and earth greets,
During sun's reign darkness in retreat,
Day break stepping into morning,
Colours on earth soon be adorning.

At dawn, if clouds don't deny,
If there is a clear blue sky,
Sun seen, slowly, climbing high,
When stars and the moon give way,
Witness sunrise ushering a new day.

Time stepping into working hour,
Rhythm of life begins to power,
Following sleep and slumber
Human and wild life awakening,
Door to a new day is opening.

30.04.2014

DUAL CORE

Depiction in duality of senses
And opposite experiences,
Reason, rationale and relativity,
Cognition, conception and sensitivity,
Cause and effect sense after and before,
All senses perceived in dual core.

Perception pictured, image stored,
Image to memory restored,
Cause and effect rooting into reason,
Reasons rising to will then into volition,
With reactions in results actions entwined,
In perpetuating paradoxes answers outlined.

Two way channel of communication
Of speech, hearing and co-ordination,
Eyes to see and beauty to behold,
Darkness into light for sights to unfold,
Two gender code seeding life in existence,
Binary codes feeding artificial intelligence.

Radiance and aesthetic purity of beauty
Unimaginable as an absolute entity,
Duality in her breath anxiously wavering;
At conception's perimeter un-conquering
Potency of ugly and it's wilful co-existence
Within perception's touching distance.

To be and not to be in mutual deliberation,
High and low, common core, contrasting disposition,
Long and short in a linear co-relation,
Difficult and easy in a co-relating connotation,
Before and after moving in mutual sequence,
Full and empty are in opposite congenial presence.

Light and shade born of same source,
Same head following different course.
Good and evil evidently distant and disparate,
Yet, perception's perimeter refusing to separate.
Pleasure perpetual measuring in vain,
Measuring rod calibrated in pain.

Crying freedom, wanting to be free,
Price tagged, expecting responsibility!
Without followers fame risks losing name,
Two sides needing each other, like a game;
Winners and losers share life and join
Tossing between two sides of a coin.

The power of the throne
Not the monarch's alone,
People power behind the seat
Or people cruelly muted in defeat;
One power, two extremes pulling
Connecting the ruled and those ruling.

Predator's survival, a prey killed,
A process wild nature instilled,
Survival of those fortunate fittest
And domination of the strongest;
One life lost and one gained,
A sacred order, thus, profaned.

Man's shiny path of progress,
Seemingly, looking into a bright future,
Clearly at a cost that transgress,
Contaminating purity of nature;
In dual core of progressive action
Price of progress paid in pollution.

When they met, fate and fortune,
Together they played two way tune,
Feeling good or feeling bad,
Singing happy or sighing sad.
Necessity looking for a co-relation
Finally, met mother of invention.

Love in touching distance of hate,
Extremes of volatile emotional state,
Two dwellers inhabiting one heart,
Time and emotions setting them apart.
Strong measurably upstaged the weak,
That measure, the link, seeking the peak.

Natural phenomena of force of gravity,
Of electromagnetic field, of relativity,
Progeny of electro-magnetic fusion
In light's luminous creative elocution,
Gravity and it's innate dynamic force
Dictating masses their position and course.

Sun's energy and light adding sight,
Ocean's progenitive creative might,
Co-relating contribution of sun and sea
Holding secrets of life in a golden key
In the process of weather formation
Unlocking seeds of life, secrets of creation.

Earth's orbit into darkness and light,
Interplay of twenty four hours of day and night,
Progeny of positive and negative intercourse,
Birth of electricity, a potent power source,
Every action coded in a body of reaction,
Life's dynamics in a core of energy and motion.

Without motion time standing still – inaction
For human cognition, perception and deduction.
Energy leasing life into actions in motion,
A body and a brain in a dual core action,
A beginning and an end – life and death,
Opposite ends of one life, first to last breath.

11.12.2014

ESSENCE OF CREATION

In a maze of paradoxes of conflicting emotions,
In a passage of time seeking answers and solutions,
Mortality the absolute, the essence of creation;
A purposeful process of sustained elimination,
A natural connotation, a rational configuration.

Facing mortality, one way journey, time transient,
A gift of longer life by a medical science subservient;
Living in a quandary, choosing or losing dignity,
Be a burden, breaking the back of welfare society,
Fruitless existence or an early quietus of a life of quality.

Measuring life by mere length of time lived
Or, by the breadth of actions and results achieved;
In care, in an apparent cage, all purpose faded,
Living dead, unable to function unaided,
A blessing or a curse, paradoxically coded.

Population explosion's fall outs emerging in the equation
As rivers, oceans and atmosphere choking in pollution;
If, life defied death and the process of elimination,
Denying the beauty and essence of creation,
Human temptation, thus, unsettling natural calibration.

Science clearly challenging the inevitable feared,
As, a long life, dream of immortality, universally desired,
Potentially purpose defeating, yet, widely aspired;
Mortality, divinely designed, meaningfully measured,
Reason why life sensed beautiful and treasured!

27.08.2014

FACE

Whether evolving from distant ancestral ape
Or, reflecting image of a divine shape,
A human face nature uniquely designed,
A mirror reflecting each individual mind;
The young reflecting energy, beauty and vitality,
The old depicting time's imprint, frailty and mortality.

When at a glance two faces first meet,
Strangers, but, eyes tenderly greet,
As Eros with his arrows duly aims
Two lonely hearts love truly claims;
No words spoken, but, intent and bracing
To be in each other's arms embracing.

A face familiar, a family member or a friend,
A bond, an attachment to the end,
Yearning for faces that endeared,
At times of separation loneliness feared,
A face that lights up at the thought of union,
A face that darkens at the loss of a dear one.

A funny face of a comic or a clown
In laughter transforming a frown,
Faces of emotional eloquence of actors
Enacting multitude of imaginary characters,
Actors portraying many faces on stage,
Actors in real life deliberately engage.

A fighting soldier's expressive war torn face,
In contrast, a pious priest's face of calm and grace,
An aggressor's ferocious and fiery gesture
Reflecting on victim's fearful facial texture,
A winner proud or modest elated in own glory,
A loser downhearted, another face of same story.

At work facing an animated, infallible, egoistic boss,
Not a pretty face, but, following orders fearing job loss.
Politicians appearing in parliament engaged in a debate
Elated, expressing points of view in matters of state.
In court, face of justice, judge in a wig, authority to impress;
In sport as in court, winning crowd cheer at loser's distress.

Kings and queens in faces of crowned glory,
Why crowds cheer? That's another story.
Face of knowledge, an academic, a teacher,
Clergy in cassock a reverend preacher,
Police in uniform, face of law and order,
Drunken souls on the streets, impressions of disorder.

Words on occasion breach and betray,
Reflections on a face, a true picture portray,
Intentions naked hue clearly express
Motives behind that may transgress,
The vile look of pleasure inflicting pain,
Most unsightly face of cruelty and disdain.

Looks that transmit cruelty and fear,
Looks that charity and kindness endear,
Looks of affluence and prosperity,
Looks of modesty and humility,
Looks of arrogance of power and pride,
Looks that's repressive and chillingly chide.

Faces of masked make-up or made up in style,
None can match those glowing in a smile;
Lifting spirit, shackled in cosmetic buys,
Attracting many admiring passing eyes,
Fallen victims to cruel knives of plastic surgery
In costly curving of fake and forged imagery.

Faceless power of a multinational corporation
A formidable feature in a quiet revolution,
Greed goblins global game plan and gambits,
Faceless head counts sacrificing jobs for profits.
Forced into perimeter of progressive automation
Are we powerless witness to a phased dehumanisation?

A face, a unique form of identity,
Characteristic emblem of a human society
Some we may fall in love at first sight,
Some, terrifying, we scream at in a fright.
Face to face let's enlighten and embrace
Fair, dark or brown, one unique human race.

10.03.2014

FIRST LOVE

A man and a woman entering cupid's den,
Dormant love awakening when
Two strangers meet at a glance,
Eyes greet then tenderly advance.

Cupid, positively aimed his darts,
Piercing into two ecstatic hearts,
Fallen and intent, each clearly affirms
Embracing into each other's arms.

That scintillating spark of resolve,
That unconquerable flame of love
Blind to all barriers, a burning fire,
A sacred flame of pure desire.

Kindled fire of rapturous delight,
Enchantment in a wondrous flight,
In a journey where two paths converging,
Where two hearts into one emerging.

23.12.2015

FORGIVENESS

When phantom fate blindly strikes a poison dart,
A maze of thought clouds and reasons ripped apart.
Coping with an unpleasant event, a tragedy and torment
Of an irretrievable loss, a reminder every living moment;
Two thoughts conflict with equal chance,
Reasoned acceptance or vowed vengeance.

Powerless to reclaim fates feral forfeiture,
Cherish happy memories, looking into future,
Or, continue to carry a life long heavy burden,
A grief or a guilt that perpetuate and harden.
Vengeful 'tit for tat', yet another poison dart
Determined to inflict, refusing to part.

Only searing victim, no cheering victor,
As an extra-ordinary power over the perpetrator
Victims only road to liberation is ability to forgive,
Rising above in a powerful release of cocooned plaintive.
Forgiveness may fulfil life in fortitude, a delicate art,
Pure and positive, painted in a forgiving heart.

02.09.2014

FORTUNE FAVOURED AT BIRTH

Those privileged by birth
Inheriting big chunks of the earth,
Wielding all material stronghold.
If, underprivileged aspire, they are told
To restrain and refrain from actions bold,
Recourse to justice only at a price sold.

Course ahead, lodging a pitiful protest,
Daring for a fair hearing at best,
Any stronger dubbed anarchy,
Pinned down by heavy handed hierarchy.
Privileged destined to dream and desire,
Proletarians may dream, not to aspire.

A pricked conscience branded 'left',
Left out by fists firmly clenched;
Another version reads 'red',
'Red light' to stop aspirations dead.
All joined hands to grow fruits of labour,
Distribution distorted in fortune's favour.

Absorbed in power of wealth and assumed nobility,
Suffocating noble power of egalitarian mobility,
Implore imperatives of narrowing the widening gap,
Picture potentials and possibilities of a new map,
A mirage of wasteful greed distorting unsightly gloom,
Let in the sunshine, watch it bloom, watch it bloom!

Lost in a whirlwind of power and pelf,
Submerged in a glory sodden self,
Ignorance of power of a helping hand,
A grand gesture, a noble stand,
Living in fond memory in peoples' heart,
World a better place learning this simple art.

15.12.2014

FOUR SEASONS

Seasonal brushes painting
Many faces of nature,
Sketches of splashing colours
In framed picture.

Spring – nature's awakening hour,
Romantic hour, begins to flower,
Cattle grazing, sheep lambing – progenitive.
Summer – working hour, flowers to fruits,
Generating seeds, extending roots,
Snow caps melting, green, playful – prerogative.
Autumn – harvest time, filling the granaries,
Changing attires, moving sceneries,
Colours fading – ready for repose.
Winter – dormant, sleeping and slumbering hour,
In this blissful earthly bower,
Frozen, snow capped – doors close.

An admixture of
Earthly colour and sunlight
In earth's passages
From annual orbital flight.

16.11.2014

HOPE

When adversity starkly staring,
I am losing all control and bearing,
Whole world ahead seem very dark,
Needing a glimmer of light, a spark!

Hope is that glimmer and flame of life
That lights up the dark alley of strife,
Beyond that adversity closed chapter and page,
Only, radiance of strength and courage.

Followed by expectations, no limitation,
Raised aspirations, even a little temptation!
Tomorrow, today will step into yesterday,
Rain clouds will give way to a sunny day.

31.12.2014

IF ONLY

If only, sunshine and showers evenly measured
And treasured harvest evenly shared,
If only, poverty didn't play a part in this life,
Terminated disease, hardship and strife.

If only beauty prevailed on earth,
Ugliness was never granted it's birth,
If only, pain had never played a part,
Sensed prolonged pleasure by a blissful art.

If only, love was allowed to rule every heart
And hate from earth for good did depart,
If only, We didn't engage in raging war
Peace, though, we all prefer by far.

If only, good in perpetuity prevailed,
Evil never given a chance and failed,
If only, knowledge enlightened every soul
And ignorance pushed forever in a dark hole.

If only, youth adorned life eternally,
Age didn't cripple and end life finally,
If only, my wish was written by a Divine pen
Life would seem, then, nearer to Heaven!

08.02.1987

LIFESPAN

Nature generously provides,
Man selfishly divides,
Strong takes lion's share,
Weak, for fear of fight, may not dare,
For peace, accepts a share unfair.

Knowledge reveals what's in store,
Strong grabs more and more,
Then, tries to shut the door,
Knowledge keeps door open as before,
Given opportunity, weak may yet explore.

Love's lesson is compromise,
Peaceful co-existence a fair prize,
Strong's greed has no limit or size,
Weak may be meek seeks life's bliss
In love, contentment and peace.

Time's tenure is strict to the rule,
Strong and weak both allowed in full,
Actions good or evil time will reveal,
Actions good may be allowed a fair deal,
For many, sadly, fate fortuitously seal.

Death the redeemer,
The ultimate schemer,
The inevitable leveller,
At life's end waiting to strike,
Dust to dust, strong and weak alike.

19.08.2014

MAN AND MACHINE

Man's brainchild born a machine,
With artificial intelligence akin,
Now, growing up in keen contest,
Challenging man for survival of the fittest!
Man of lower skill may very well sense
Outwitted by artificial intelligence;
Man under stronghold of his own prodigy
But, man-made machines making no apology.

Machines sharing burden of hardship with man
That's how all began with an innovative plan,
Sparing man from his back breaking toil
In forests, mines, constructions and tilling soil;
Now, on farmland spraying pesticides killing pests,
Combined harvesters reaping bumper harvests;
Trawlers netting bigger catch while fishing
And while at sea fewer lives lost and missing.

Humanity now facing fewer famines, better fed,
Longer healthier life and fewer dead.
Ever faster land, water and air transport,
Since the birth of family car and home comfort,
Hives of global economic and trading activity
Sharing fruits of productivity and prosperity;
But, as consumer led economy pitching sale
Caution! earth's finite resources tipping the scale.

Man the mastermind, the innovator
Began life with small tools and cultivator,
Landed on the moon, a fantasy fulfilled,
Giant telescopes looking into farther afield;
Communication satellites, weather eyes,
Remote drones and intelligence gathering spies,
Space research station in the sky hanging,
Mars probe and many others intensifying.

Diagnostic machines and surgical aids
Counting over crowded geriatric heads,
Killing machines, on the other hand,
Burying reasoned heads under the sand.
Binary reason, master of speed and precision,
Multiple decisions, immense analytical dimension,
In a process perilously preaching job stealing,
In a process dehumanisation slowly wheeling.

World wide web in a quiet revolution
Invading every home by cunning coercion,
Virtually all daily routine human actions
Translating into online transactions.
Miracle of the little mobile phone in hand
Responding to touch sensitive command;
Information technology and artificial intelligence
Virtual life blood of modern society in essence.

Society systematically drawn into formation,
Into controlled near robotic life function
Where fate is sealed by the faceless
Distant multinational corporations – heartless!
Witnessing fading human touch and emotion,
Watching entropy of feeling slowly in motion.
No longer a future fantasy of science fiction,
Already pawns in our daily slice of action.

Progress running at a galloping speed,
Blinkered, by passing basic human need,
As right to work being shovelled in scrap heap,
Irony in picture potential probing deep.
Jobs shedding day by day and heads rolling,
Man's brainchild now quietly controlling
Agriculture, manufacture and infrastructure,
Trend setting socio-economic culture.

In strong grip of artificial intelligence
For day to day dependence and reliance
Unaided, national grid will fail, aircrafts won't fly,
Transports will stand still, water taps will run dry,
Supermarket shelves will be empty, won't fill
Banks will breach, cash machines with empty till.
Machines may falter machines may function
Man is shackles by his own creative action.

Artificial intelligence destined to flourish,
Birth of social media humanity may cherish,
Life once sensed real, enlightened human race,
In cyber world virtual man may learn to embrace;
Man pledged to breaking boundaries of knowledge,
Widening his horizon a compelling challenge,
The mastermind of imaginations still holding the key,
How calamitous losing control would be?

Continuing globalization and quiet cyber revolution
Culminating cross culture communication and
evaluation,
Harvesting growing fruits of human knowledge tree,
Sadly, slowly pulverising family cohesion and
community;
While reaping harvest of fruitful human innovations
Rooting, in parallel, hazards of weeds' indubitable
motivations,
Facing a challenge, maintaining a fine line of balance
Between fall outs of evil and pinnacle of excellence.

10.11.2015

MY LOVE FOR YOU

That moment when I first set my eyes on you I then knew
That never again I would like to part company from you,
I treasure till this day the spark and tingle of your first kiss,
Pleasure of your company always is an unparalleled bliss.

My love for you is deeper than the deepest ocean bed
And higher than the highest mountain head,
Warmer than the warm welcoming sun at advent of Spring,
Fresher than the freshness that morning dews bring.

My love for you is tender as the tenderest flower petals,
Stronger than the strongest of all strong metals,
As pure as day break embracing morning sunlight
And as true as the sun promised day and night.

I live to see you always happy, content and smiling,
It hurts deep if I ever hurt you not knowing,
No music sounds sweeter than sound of your laughter,
My love for you promised till my last breath falter.

23.12.2015

OCEAN

The sea and the ocean beyond, solitude bound,
In restless motion, spirituality in silence and sound,
Tranquillity under wide open sky and space,
That sense of solitude every man's embrace.

Breaking waves lapping the shores under sky's watchful eyes,
At ebb lying low, rising as tides flow, windswept riding high.
Sun and sea unlocked secrets of life by a divine decree,
Together, trusted keepers of a secret celestial key.

In a unique weather cycle, trinity of ocean, wind and sun,
Clouds form, then rain falls, in turn lakes fill and rivers run.
Passive moon quietly in action along with the forceful trinity,
Twice daily, high and ebb tides conforming lunar line of gravity.

Countless falls, rapids, streams, brooks rills and rivers
Travelling across earth's every remote corners
Rushing back towards estuaries to the sea and the ocean
Replenishing and revitalising in a timeless energising
motion.

Rugged rock faced strands, beaches of golden sand,
Dotted with many islands, ocean that shaped the land,
Housing coral reefs, kelp forests and supporting marine lives,
Flow of currents and temperature, weather pattern scribes.

Vast expanse surrounding the land, a secret world in the deep
Where earth's largest inhabitants eat, drink and sleep;
Together inhabiting ancient ancestral microscopic sire,
Submerged mountain ridges and violent volcanoes
breathing fire.

Mother of first concept of life, in the deep gave birth,
Germinating seeds of all living beings on earth,
Mysteries lie in the depth of this phenomenon,
A creative motion of progenitive profusion.

Sea faring sailors' treasure trove, harvesting their bounty,
Paradoxically, a hungry grave, an epitome of cruelty,
Hidden heritage, nameless, numberless, concealed graves,
Silent witness, sleeping beneath the restless waves.

A reservoir of unlimited goodness in decline
From man's folly that's challenging the divine;
Poison filled by pollution, nature is in dumb disillusion
By man's commercial servitude, a greed filled illusion.

Man's success story, a miracle in the mist,
The purity nature lost submerged in an ethical twist.
Once a peaceful sanctuary of pure serene solitude
Reshaping in matters metamorphosis of material magnitude.

28.11.2015

PATH FINDERS

For most, do as others do, daren't defy,
Following the herd then happy to die.
A select few dare to question why?

Seeking knowledge for an answer,
Travelling near and far to discover,
Breaking boundaries they do dare.

Prejudices fearlessly fight,
Fears of the unknown given sight,
Darkness of ignorance given light.

Beyond boundaries in their vision
Widening humanity's horizon,
Pathfinders proliferating civilization.

24.11.2015

PEACE CONUNDRUM

Why do we go to war
In the name of peace?

And why do we act dishonourably
In the name of honour?

More than often to protect
Individual pride and prejudice.

The mass merely serve the master
Who in turn is slave of power.

24.02.1984

PRIVATE CITIZEN

For fame, high office and power he didn't fall,
Climbing a ladder proved steep and slippery,
Conflict and compromise forever stall
Promise of progress, derailed by glory sodden rivalry.

Freedom intact and privacy seem well heeded,
Offers a life where limelight made to lose power,
Able to extend a helping hand where needed,
Not seeking glory, content in a blissful bower.

In his actions truth and dignity always prevail,
Values dignity of labour not fortune and favours.
Love, charity and compassion never fail,
Happiest amongst family, friends and neighbours.

Position in present society may mark him small,
Power of uncompromised honesty fuels him to walk
tall.

15.11.2011

RAT RACE

Moving blinkered at an ever increasing pace
In a whirlwind, unaware, absorbed in a rat race,
Unable to share precious moments with loved ones,
Tender time to wipe a tear or two in the eyes of little
ones.

In haste a tender word to a loved one forgotten,
In pursuit of work that is performance trodden,
In gripping uncertainties, in constant apprehension,
Intruding restful sacred hours with sleep deprivation.

Failing to extend a tender hand to a friend at times of
need,
Little time away from work in a charitable deed,
Away from a pursuit that's a product of greed,
A thought, an action for the deprived may heed.

Rhythm of life gaining speed and wheeling,
Emotions being muted by entropy of feeling
In a blinkered race of work and performance,
Casting shadow over sanctity of home and happiness.

16.08.2014

ROBIN REDBREAST

My little robin redbreast
In my garden in her nest,
Comes out when she sees me
From her nest in the tree.

Says 'hello, tweet, tweet, tweet',
Advancing close to my feet,
Not afraid, I am her friend
And likewise she is mine to the end.

I offer her occasional treat,
She comes close, happy to eat.
Our Spring to Autumn routine,
In cold Winter we both stay in,
Don't see her much around,
Hear occasional flutter and sound.

At the advent of Spring
I hear her again tweet and sing,
With her mate in quest,
Busy mending her nest,
Raising her offspring to her best,
My little robin redbreast!

22.09.2013

SEPTEMBER SONG

When August finally bids farewell
Between Summer's hot spell
And Winter sun's waning ember,
Autumn equinox in month of September.

A month between seasons, calm
Before the seasonal storm,
May be cool or may be warm,
Indian Summer or Autumnal norm.

I remember, I remember,
Forty three years ago in September,
I held my bride's tender hands, made a vow –
Still holding, through life's high and low.

A month when birdsongs fading away,
Fields bare following harvest day,
Granaries full, birds back in nests,
Losing Summer berries' lingering tastes.

Deserted beaches, crowds vanished,
Flowers losing colours, petals blemished,
Sun waning and casting longer shadows,
Cattles suspecting misty meadows.

Woodlands ready for changing attires
In blazing brushes of Autumn colours;
Incoming month of October drawing near,
September for a year will soon disappear.

19.09.2015

SILENT NIGHT

Silent night, not a cloud in sight,
Sky is alight, stars are sparkling,
Moon is smiling, earth is sleeping,
Sun is resting until morning light.

Santa Clause leaving Lapland
Heading for Winter wonderland
Where Santa made a secret pledge,
Rudolf the reindeer pulling the sledge.

All children in bed, in peace, sleeping
In eager anticipation and dreaming,
Father Christmas, tiptoed, beaming,
Can't wait to see joyful faces screaming
Early Christmas morning.

24.12.2015

SILENT WITNESS

So often I witness injustice,
In a shock I stand and stare,
Conscience hints to pay the price
To fight for what's judged fair.

Am I considered a coward,
In back track, in retreat,
Unscathed, reaping life's reward,
Ready to surrender, facing defeat?

One life, a gift most precious;
Avoiding life's pugnacious tricks
Would turning a blind eye be callous
As I lack ammunition to fight or fix?

The victim, a life equally precious,
Action or inaction, both with equal chance,
Two lives in contention, surmised thus
In an ambiguous dividing line of conscience.

01.09.2014

SIX SENSES OF SUCCESS

Who is learned?
One who is always learning
And sees no end.

Who is brave?
One who sees no enemies
And doesn't wish them in grave.

Who is pious?
One who sees the truth
Without any bias.

Who is rich?
One who seeks contentment
And well able to reach.

Who is honourable?
When showing due respect and honour to others
One is quite capable.

Who is seeing life in full glory?
One who is moved by the power of nature
And other's life story.

19.03.2012

SOLDIERS

Soldiers follow orders they can't defy,
They are not allowed answers why,
They are to forget fear and be brave,
In line of duty on the brink of a grave,
Some come back maimed scarred and bruised,
Having nightmares and purposes confused.

Parents, wives and children share
The brunt of anguish and fear,
Very few care to wipe their tears,
Families and friends console in prayers.
Spare them as pawns of political belligerence,
Hail them only as heroes of homeland defence.

20.08.2014

SPRING

At hedgerows' whisper and beckoning
Wild lives sense a slow, but, sure awakening,
Sheep dotted on hills and valleys seen,
Cattle out grazing on pastures green.

Migrating birds in view again and flying,
Animals call end to Winter hibernating,
Warm sunshine and occasional shower
Induce plants to foliage, bud and flower.

Losing length, slowly, long dark hours of night,
Days gaining, long, sunny, warm and bright,
White clouds floating, waving passing by
Against a wide, bright, light blue sky.

Bare trees from Winter's grip are now free
For leafy attire obsessed in a frenzied spree.
From leaves to buds then blooming flowers
In beautiful bright colours of Spring's blazing hours.

Butterflies and bees blooming flowers bring,
Birds back, flying, nesting, perched they sing,
As the Spring sun warming the frozen earth
Human and wild life share merriment and mirth.

23.03.2014

STEPPING STONES

Time lost is lost forever, not allowed to regain,
Mistakes are stepping stones not all in vain,
Born time predetermined, more can't borrow,
Let me live for present and hope for tomorrow,
Where windows of opportunities galore!
Rewards beckon for those work and explore.

Greed may entice one to a golden cage,
I would rather look up to a wandering sage!
What purpose and pleasure lies behind impunity
When achieved result is stealing others' dignity?
Should avarice be the only symbol of success,
I am not at all tempted, I must, humbly, confess.

Indeed, result of one man's greed and gain
At some stead, seem other's loss and pain.
Yet, some aiming for bewildered wealth,
Others seeking love in family and friends and good health.
Some live by example, some may preach,
Having reached contentment one is truly rich.

31.10.2011

SUMMER

Showers in April, flowers in May,
Come June, 'tis midsummer's day,
Summer sunshine, Summer breeze,
In Summer holidays life's at ease.

Parks, playing fields and village greens
Filled with echoes of laughter of children and teens,
Birds flying, resting or nesting on leafy green trees,
Blossomed flowers attracting butterflies and bees.

Families and children on holidays at leisure,
Playing on a beach an innocent pleasure,
Sea side promenades and on the golden sand,
Lovers take a stroll here hand in hand.

Farmers busy working in the field
Wishing a big and bumper yield,
Odd showers and the sun's golden ray
Help to grow the golden grain, so they pray.

Then comes harvest time expecting granaries full
Before sun dims, days trim and begin to cool;
Summer fun in Summer sun, a gift of nature
In earth's weather cycle a heart warming feature.

21.07.2014

TRANQUILLITY

Submerged in overcrowded pulsation
Of human motion, of mechanical propulsion,
Gripped in a daily whirlwind trap,
Tranquillity is a rare gift to unwrap.

May be a breath of fresh air,
Seeking serene solitude somewhere,
Listening to many voices of nature
In mountain, ocean, woodland and pasture.

Listening when mighty mountain calls
Many springs rapids and falls;
Spiritual dimension of echoing voices
As exuberant wild life rejoices.

Serene sound of waterfalls and springs
As mighty mountain merrily sings,
Many wild voices mingle in merriment,
Pure earthly joy in echoing enchantment.

Hushed woodland, in subdued sound, bustling
As birds singing and breezy leaves lazily rustling;
Ocean in solitude, singing awake or asleep
As waves, relentlessly, leap from the deep.

Life in haste, a blurred, blinkered visibility,
Clearer all round vision in tranquillity,
An uncontaminated gift of divine scheme
In solitude or in nature's hymn.

30.01.2016

TWIN BIRTH

Purest form of progenitive process,
Procreation in a pair of offsprings in progress,
Seeds of purest love in germination,
In a chamber, in mother's womb, in occupation,
For days weeks and months in anticipation,
Giving birth to a blend of beautiful creation.
A boy and a girl, twins bonded together,
Loving mother, proud father, families gather.

25.03.2014

UNDER AN OLD WILLOW TREE

Watching, sitting under an old willow tree
By a shallow river, rippling flowing free,
An adornment of verdant vernal foliage
Reflecting in clear water a sparkling image.

Sunshine on rippled water shimmering,
Young lovers, linking hands, whispering,
Wild flowers in bloom, gay and gleaming,
Wild life in bustling activities beaming.

Songbirds in a chorus, hymn to the sun they sing,
White swan, majestic, an elegant floating king,
A rowing boat, lonely, in anticipation, waiting
For someone to set free, to row and be floating.

Caressed by Spring's warm sunshine
From chill wind to gentle breeze refine,
Golden daffodils seen dancing merrily,
Spring to Summer days advancing slowly.

An old arched bridge made a solemn pledge
Hugging the two banks of a sleepy village;
Under the bridge, round the old mill,
Winding river flowing gently on a foothill.

A tranquil pastoral waterside theme
Overseen by a warm Spring sunbeam,
Life in motion, moving like a gentle breeze,
Transient, transparent, tranquil, at ease.

30.04.2014

WINTER

As Autumn waves Winter in
Days losing light at night's gain,
Sun's warmth day by day failing,
Gripped by freezing cold earth's ailing.

Looking at leafless, frozen trees,
Not in sight birds or the bees,
Farmers staring at frozen fields
Bare and barren, nothing yields.

Flowers of warm days fail to bloom
In frosty Winter's dreary gloom,
Snow showers and blizzards bite,
A panorama of colourless white.

Sculptured icicles and snowflakes,
Cold freezing wind and frozen lakes;
Frost bites then warming by fireside,
Homing in hibernation animals hide.

Some sporting crowds happily elope
To snow capped mountains and ski-slope
In a joyous, playful, Winter wonderland
As in Summer escape to sea and sand.

In Winter sun's slow waning ember
Birdsongs fading, hard to remember,
Days of Summer, warm and sun-kissed,
All seem hazy in memories mist.

Santa Claus in his golden sledge,
For children, made a novel pledge,
Reindeers and jingle bells
Heart warming fairy tales.

For the young,
Hope of Spring riding high,
For the old,
Yet another year gone by!

23.12.2013

WISH

For joy,
Like an early morning in Spring,

For laughter,
Make your joyful heart sing,

For love,
Blissfully shared every day,

For hope,
Reborn like a sunrise, each unlived day,

For happiness,
Sparkling like a sun-kissed dew.

These things and more are wished for you.

21.05.2015

www.ingramcontent.com/pod-product-compliance
Lightning Source LLC
Chambersburg PA
CBHW050428290526
45786CB00003B/1435